THIS COLORING BOOK BELONGS TO

....

Color Test Page

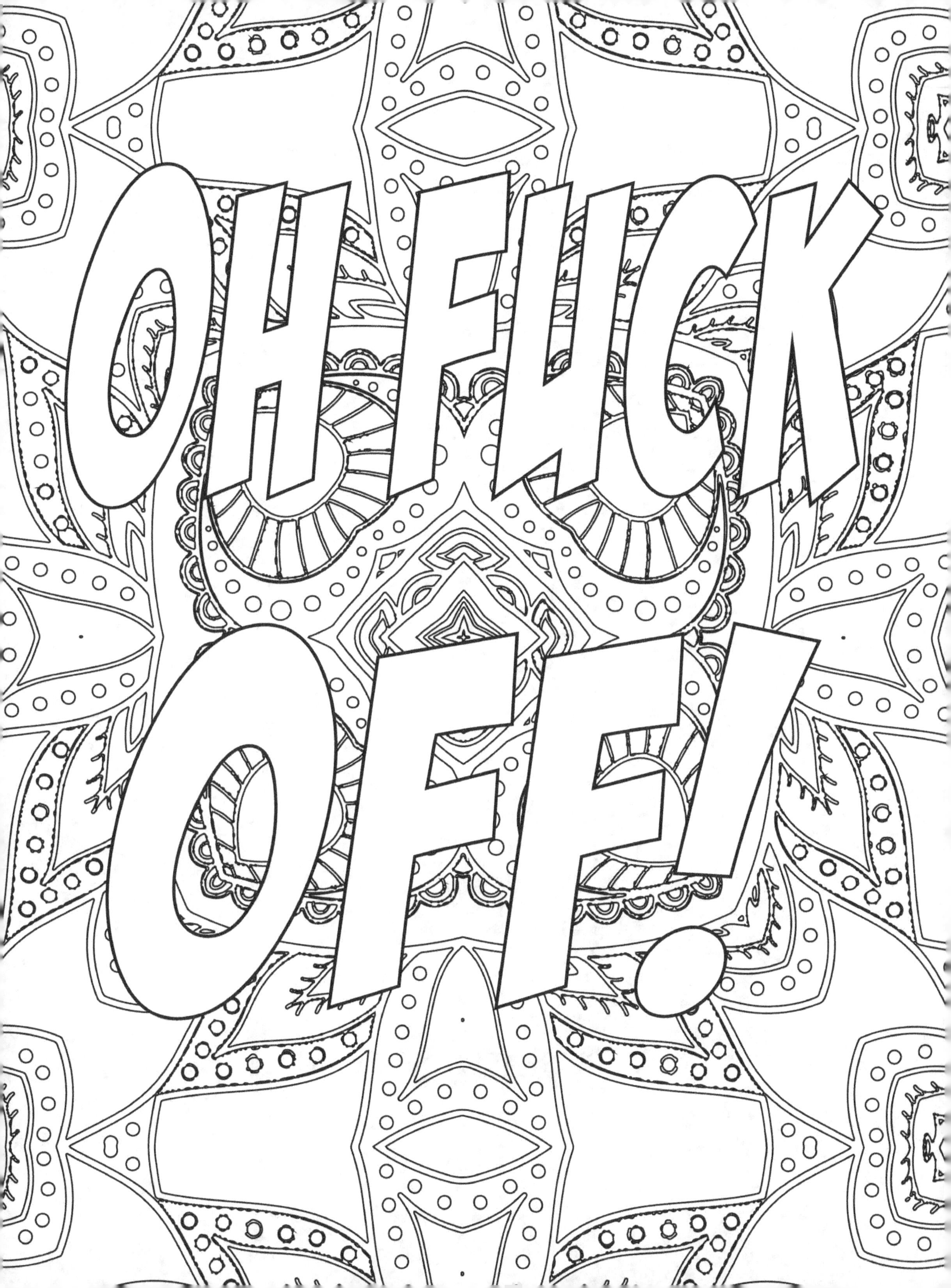
OH FUCK
OFF!

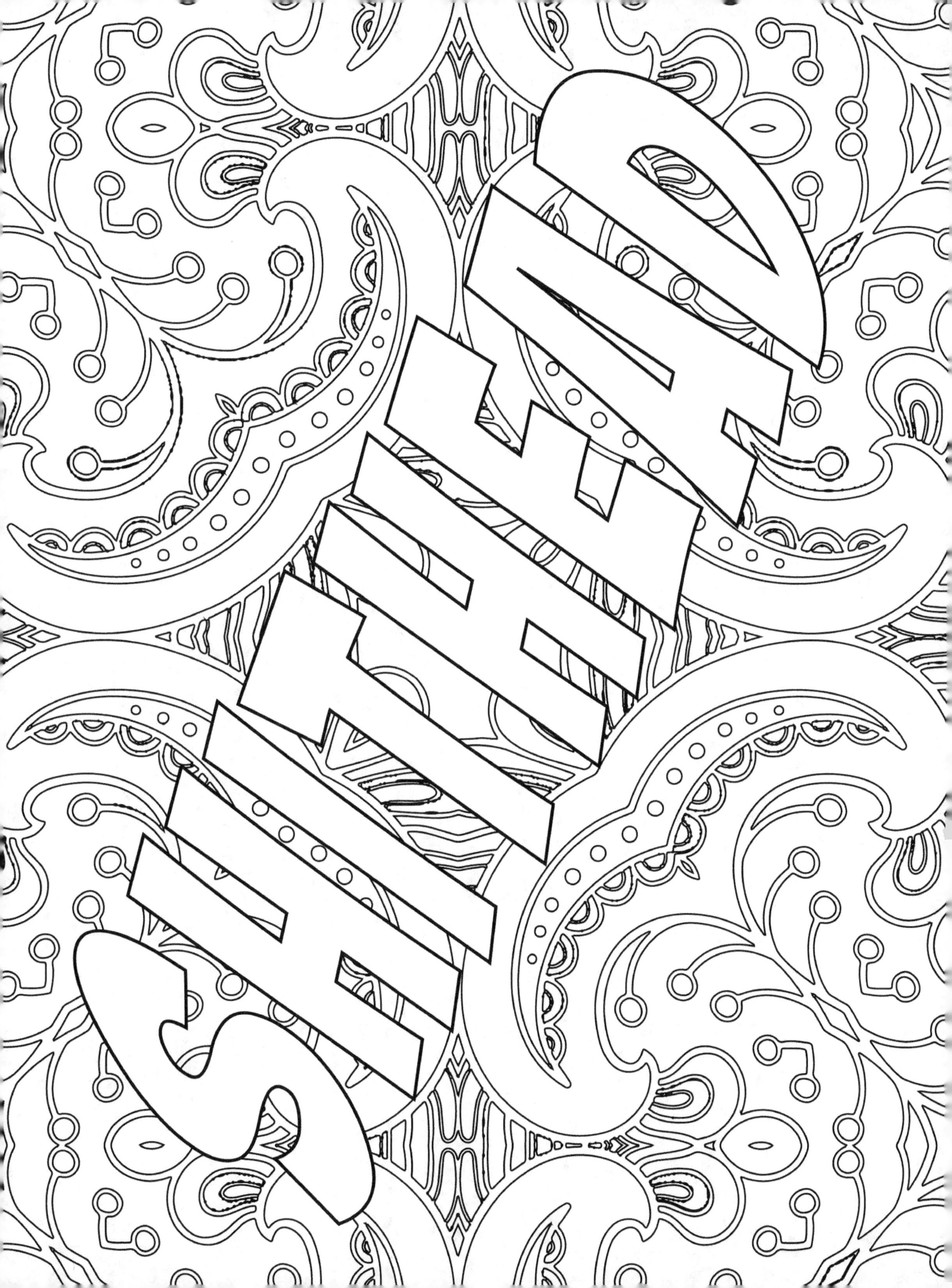
SHITHEAD

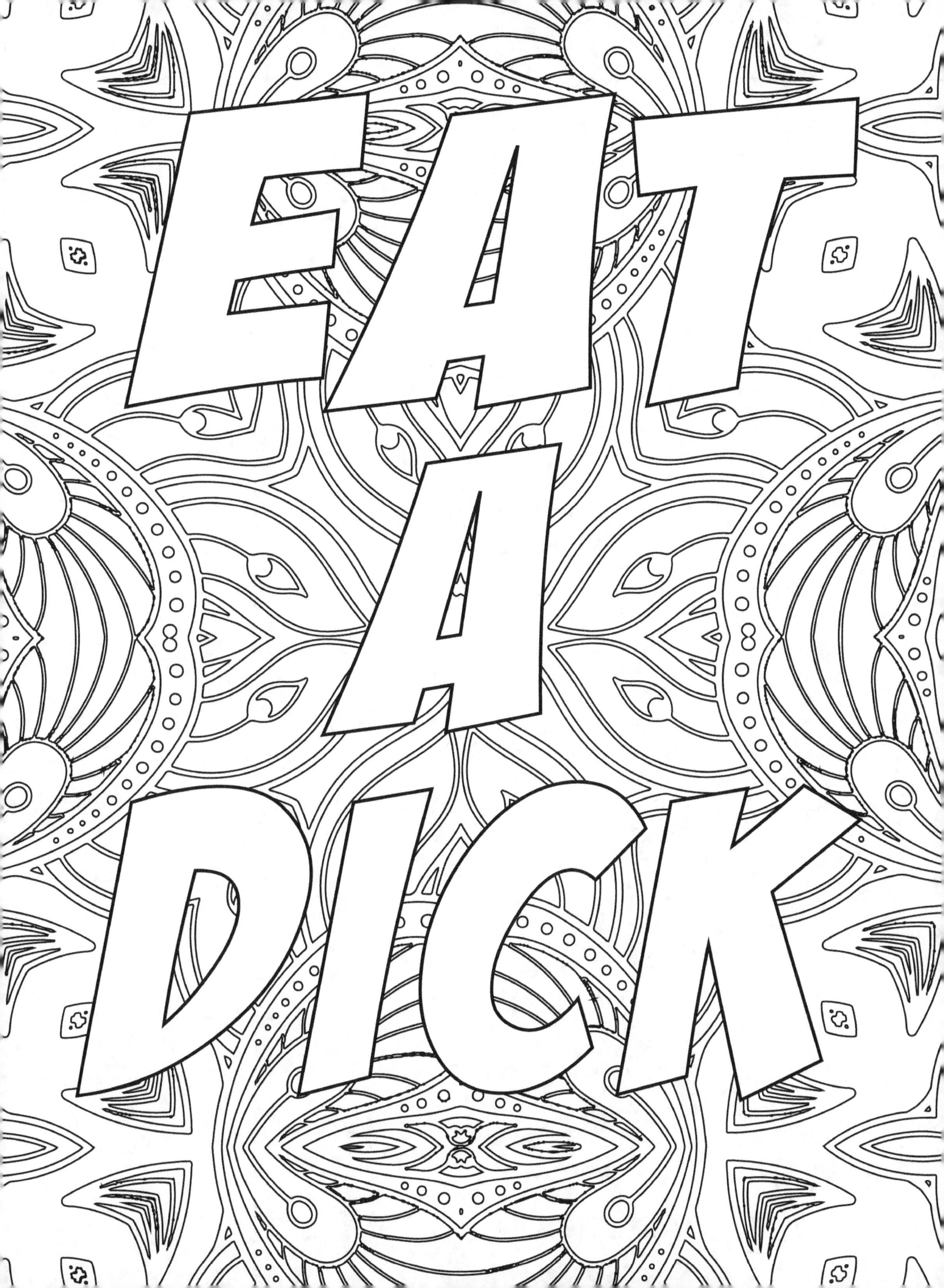
EAT
A
DICK

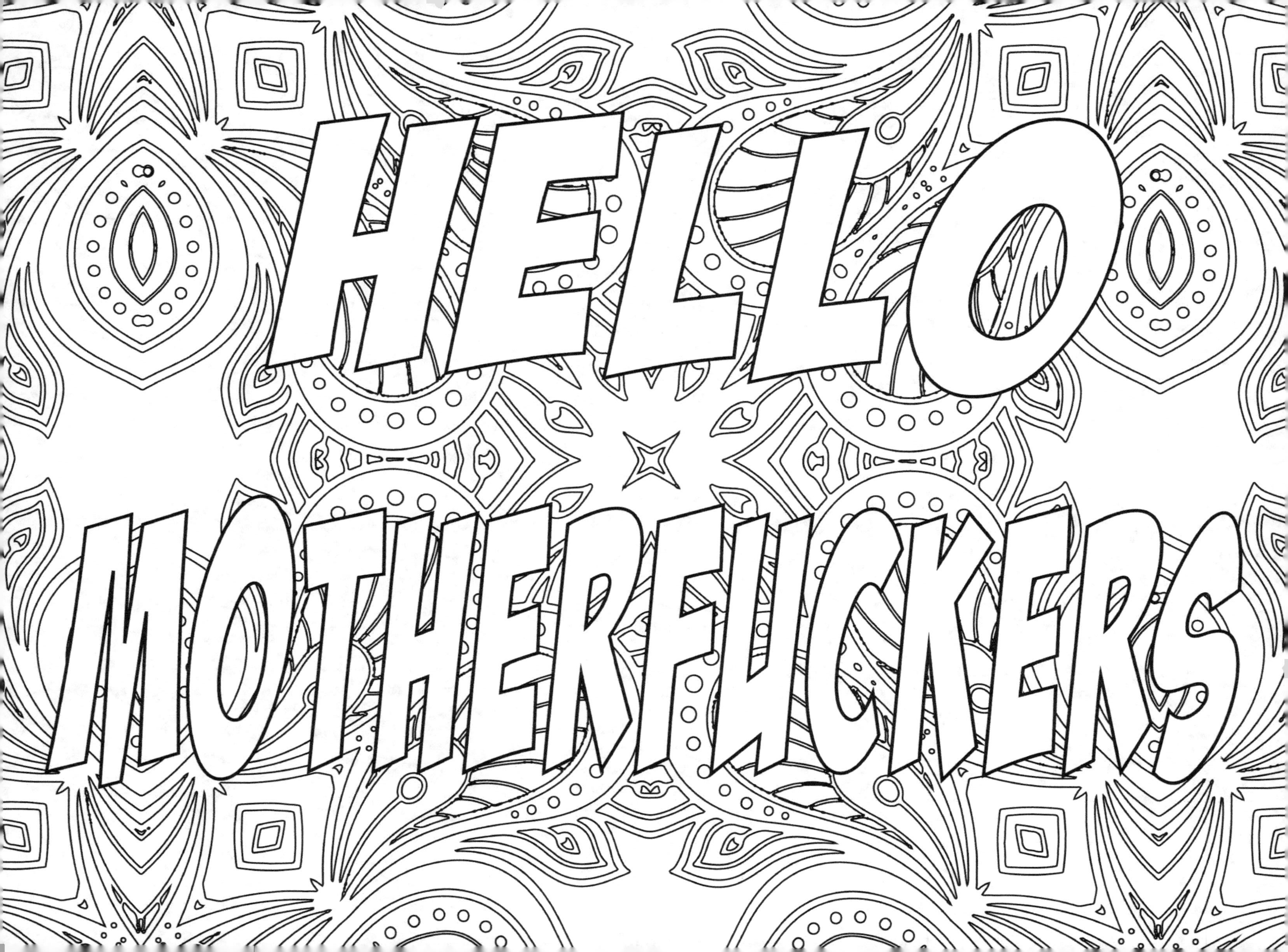
HELLO
MOTHERFUCKERS

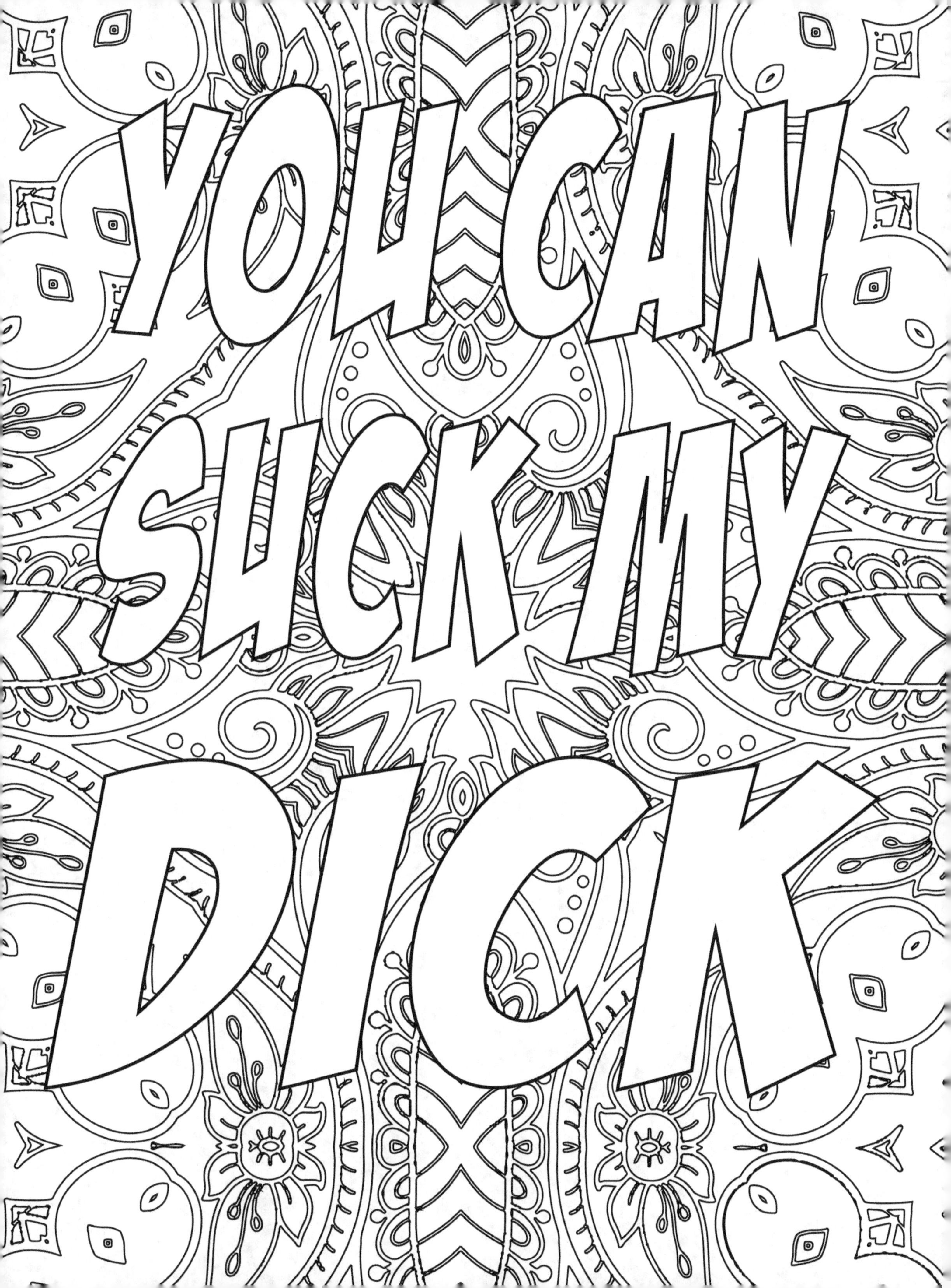
YOU CAN
SUCK MY
DICK

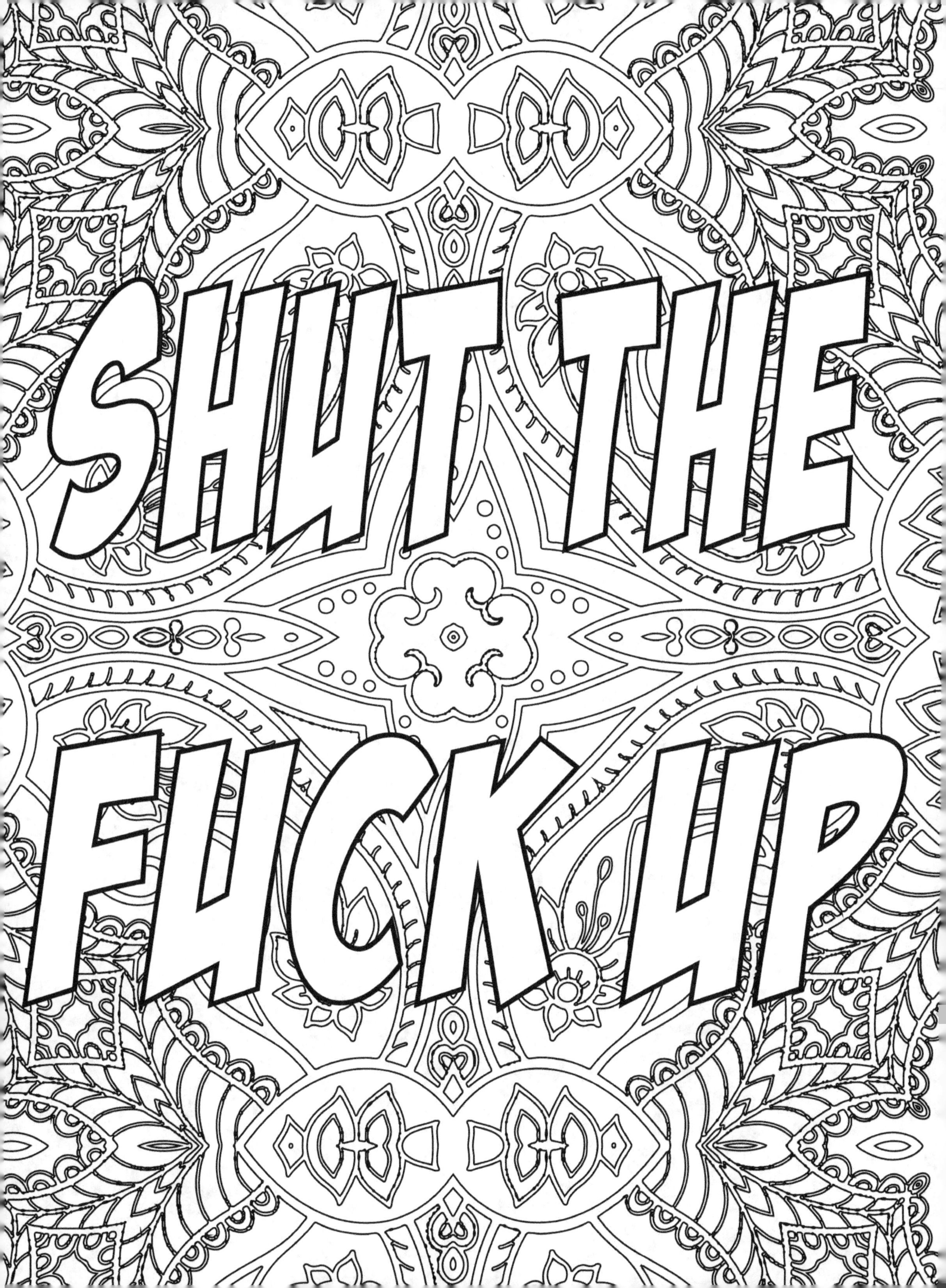
SHUT THE
FUCK UP

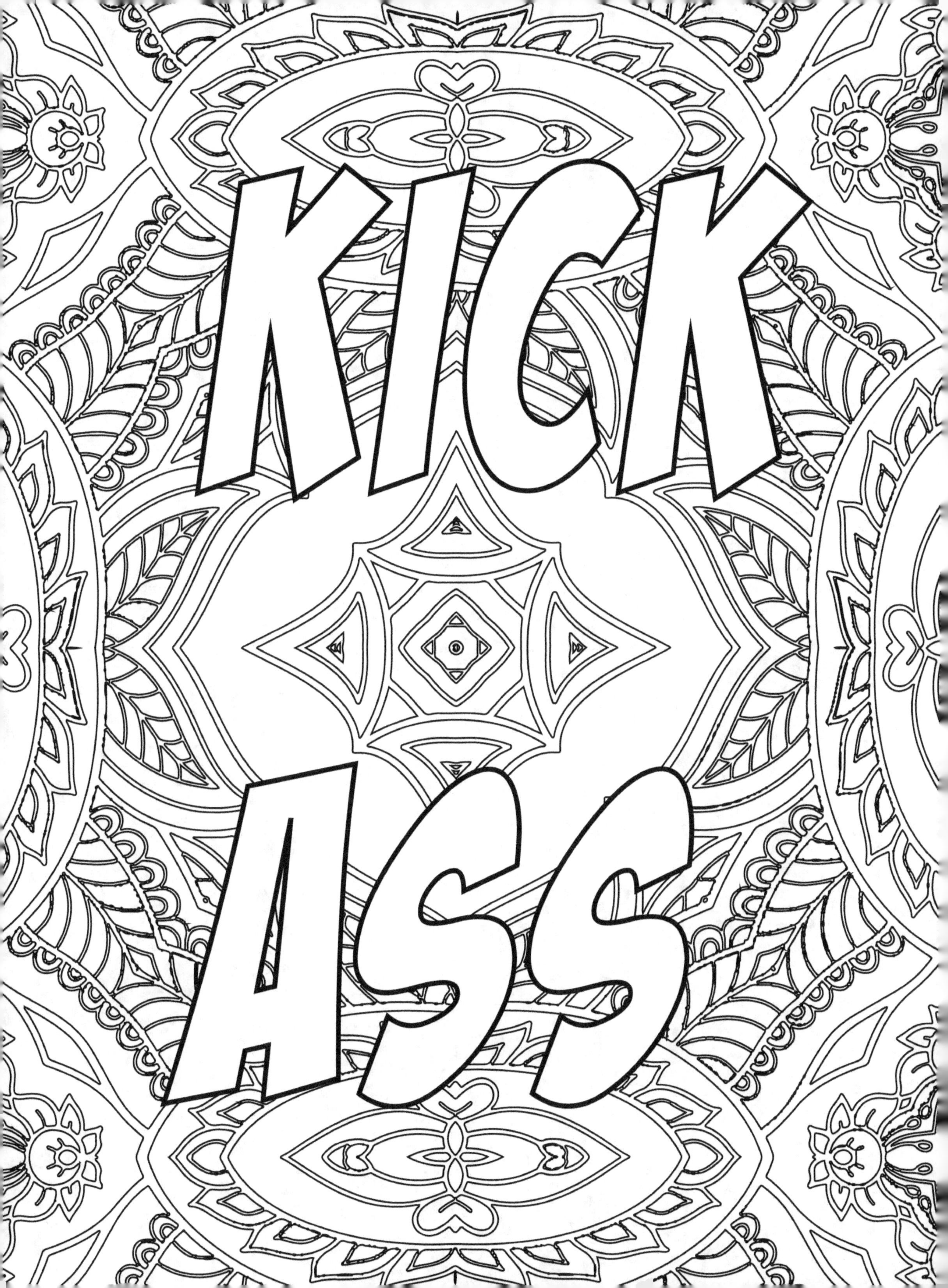
KICK
ASS

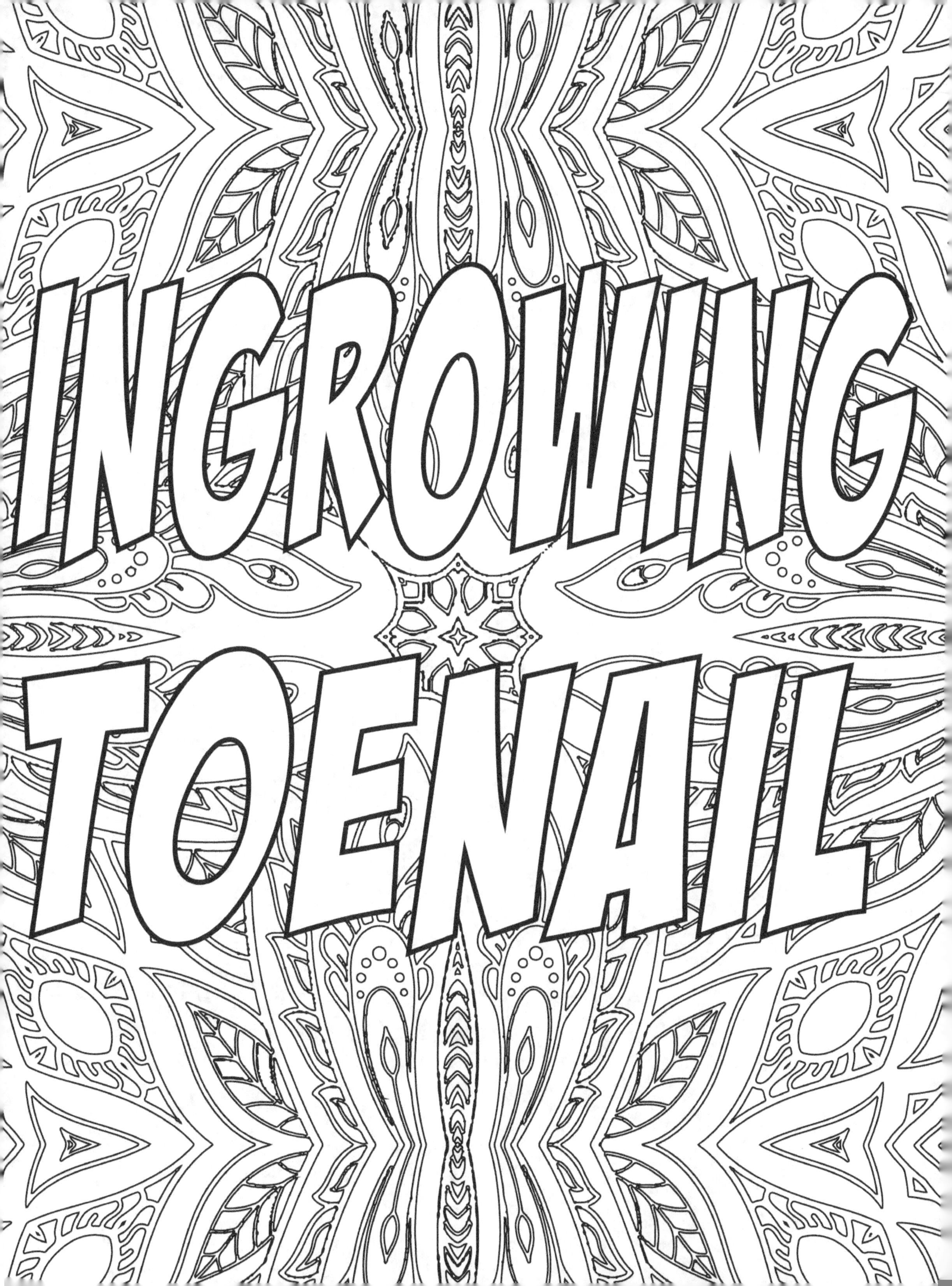
INGROWING
TOENAIL

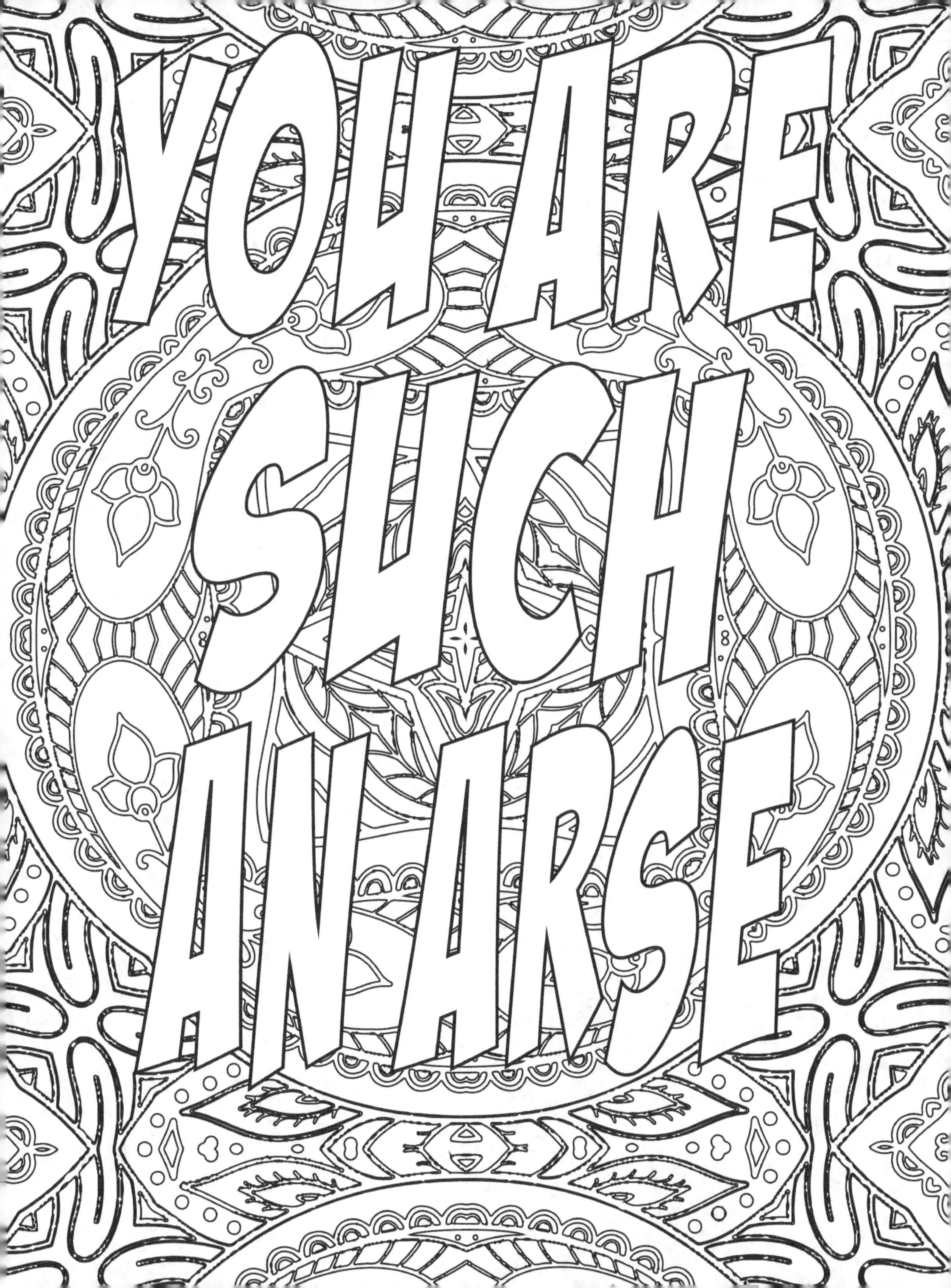
YOU ARE
SUCH
AN ARSE

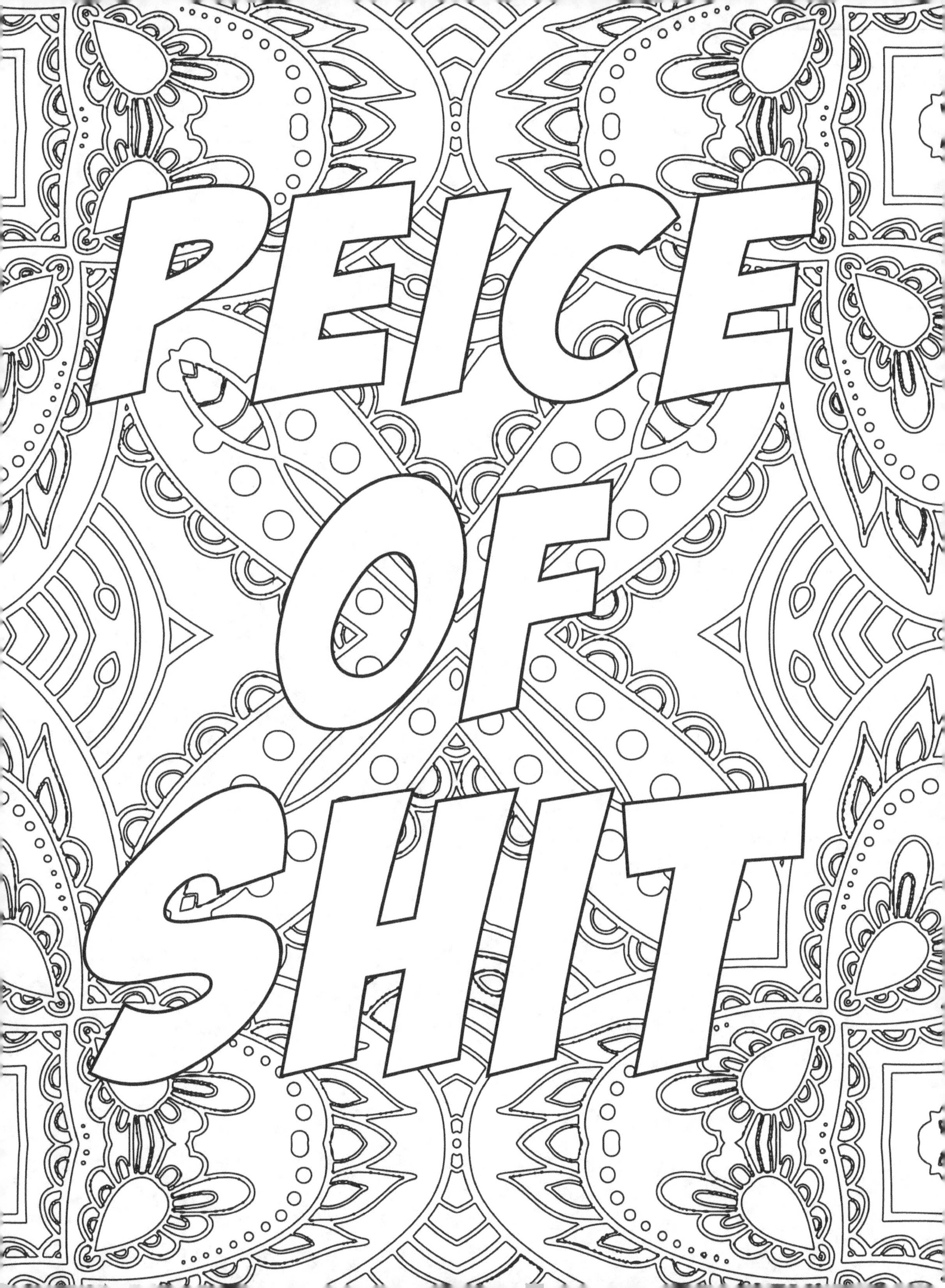
PEICE
OF
SHIT

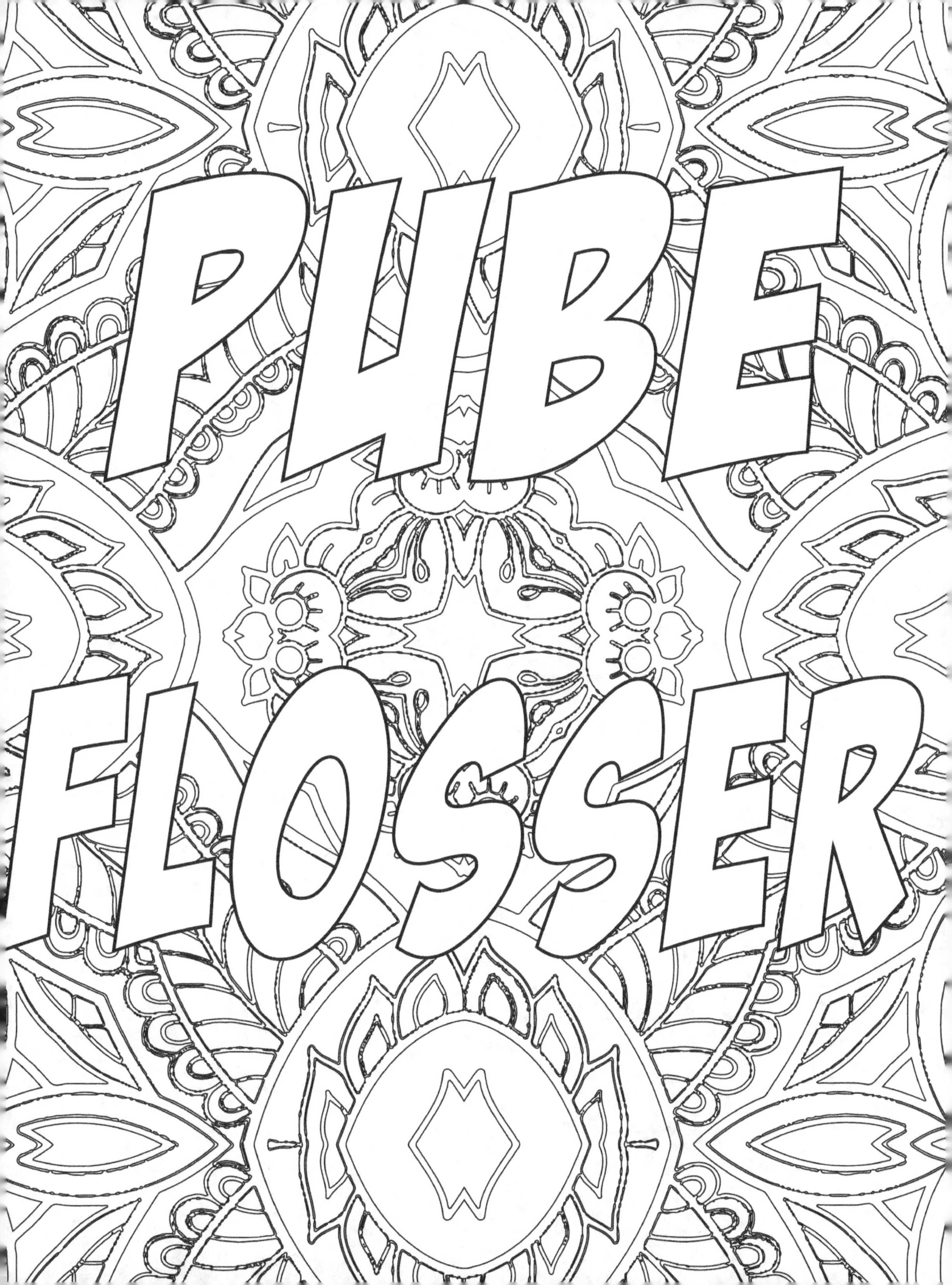
PUBE
FLOSSER

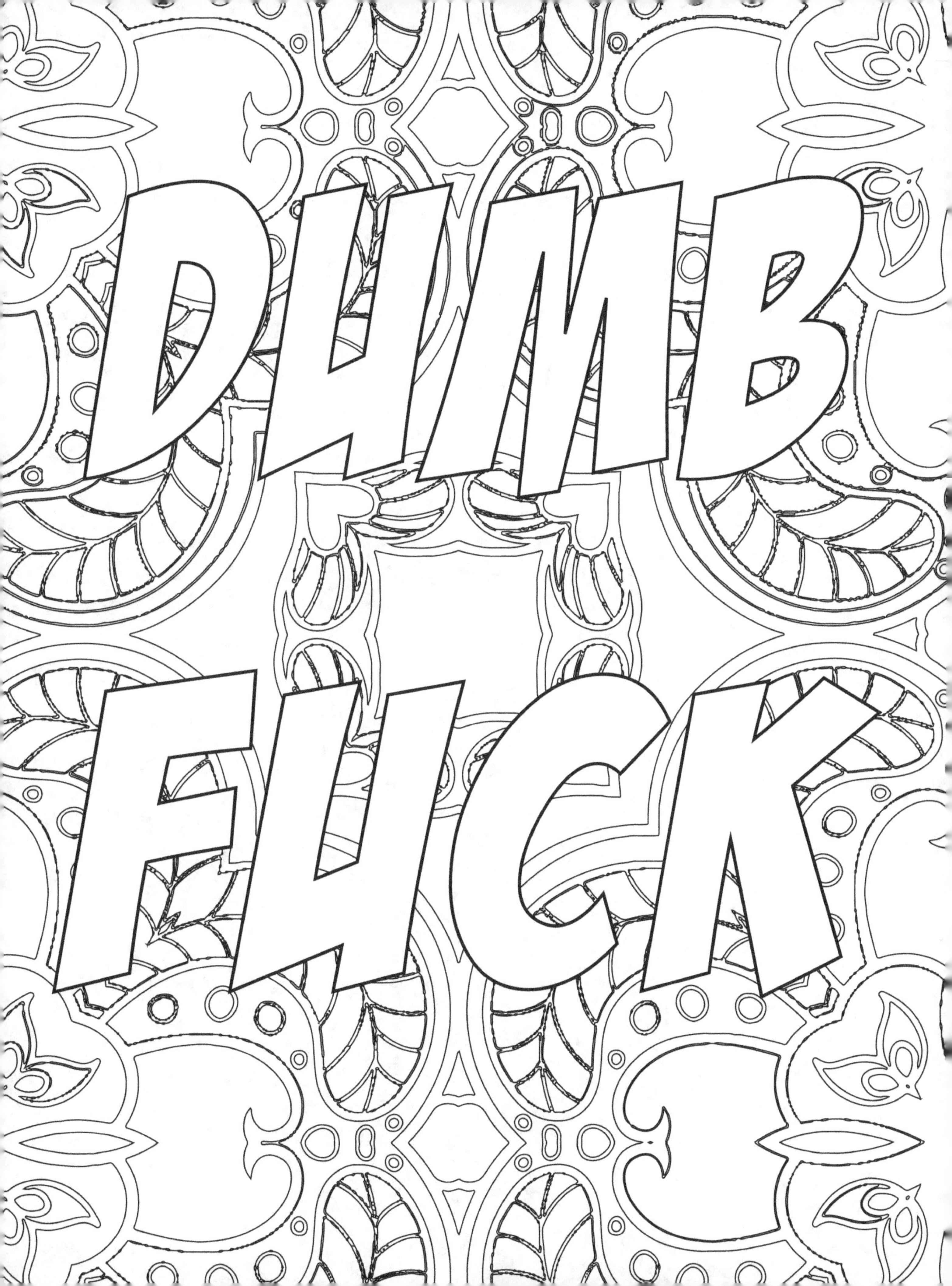
DUMB
FUCK

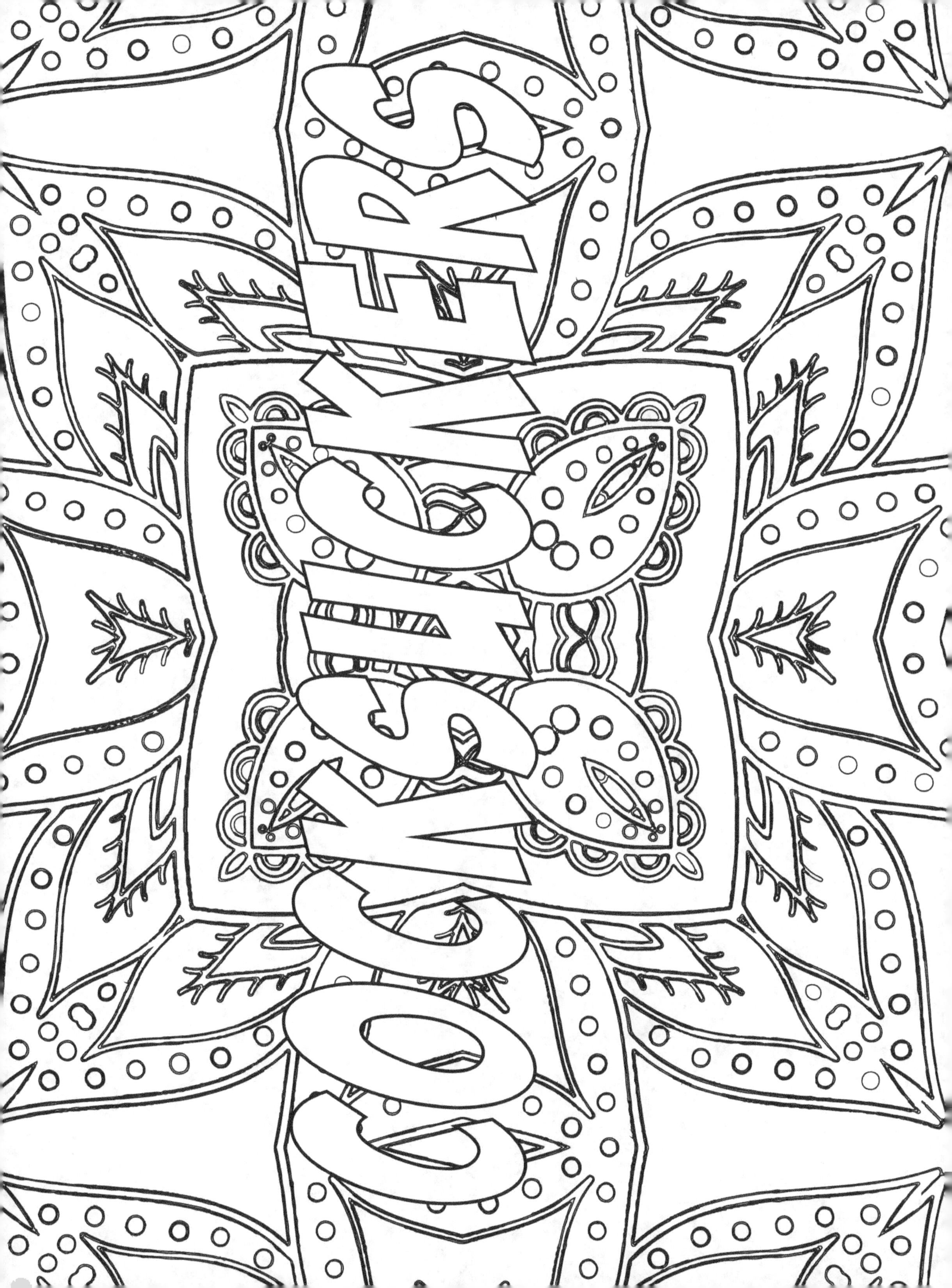
COCKSUCKERS

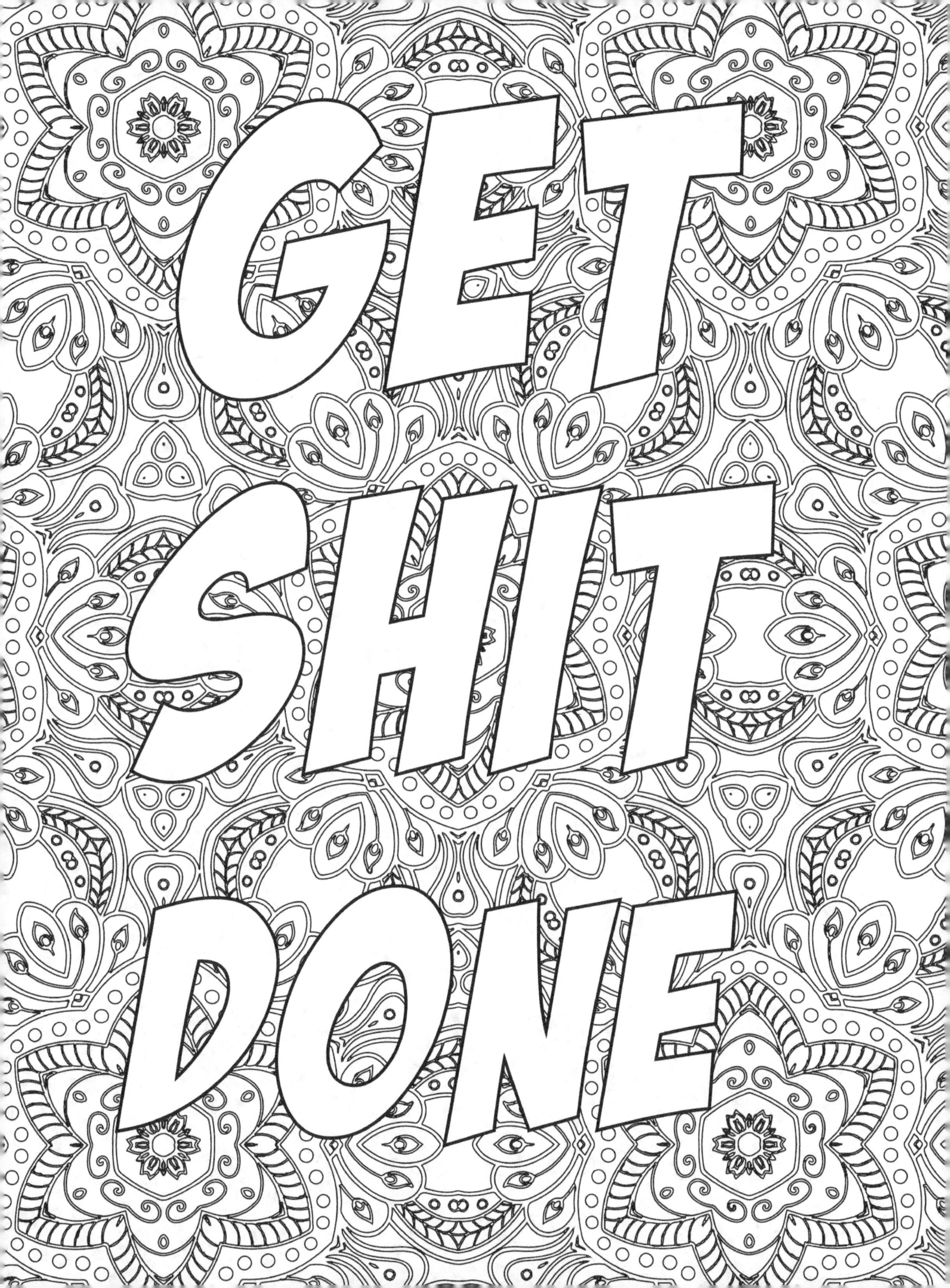
GET
SHIT
DONE

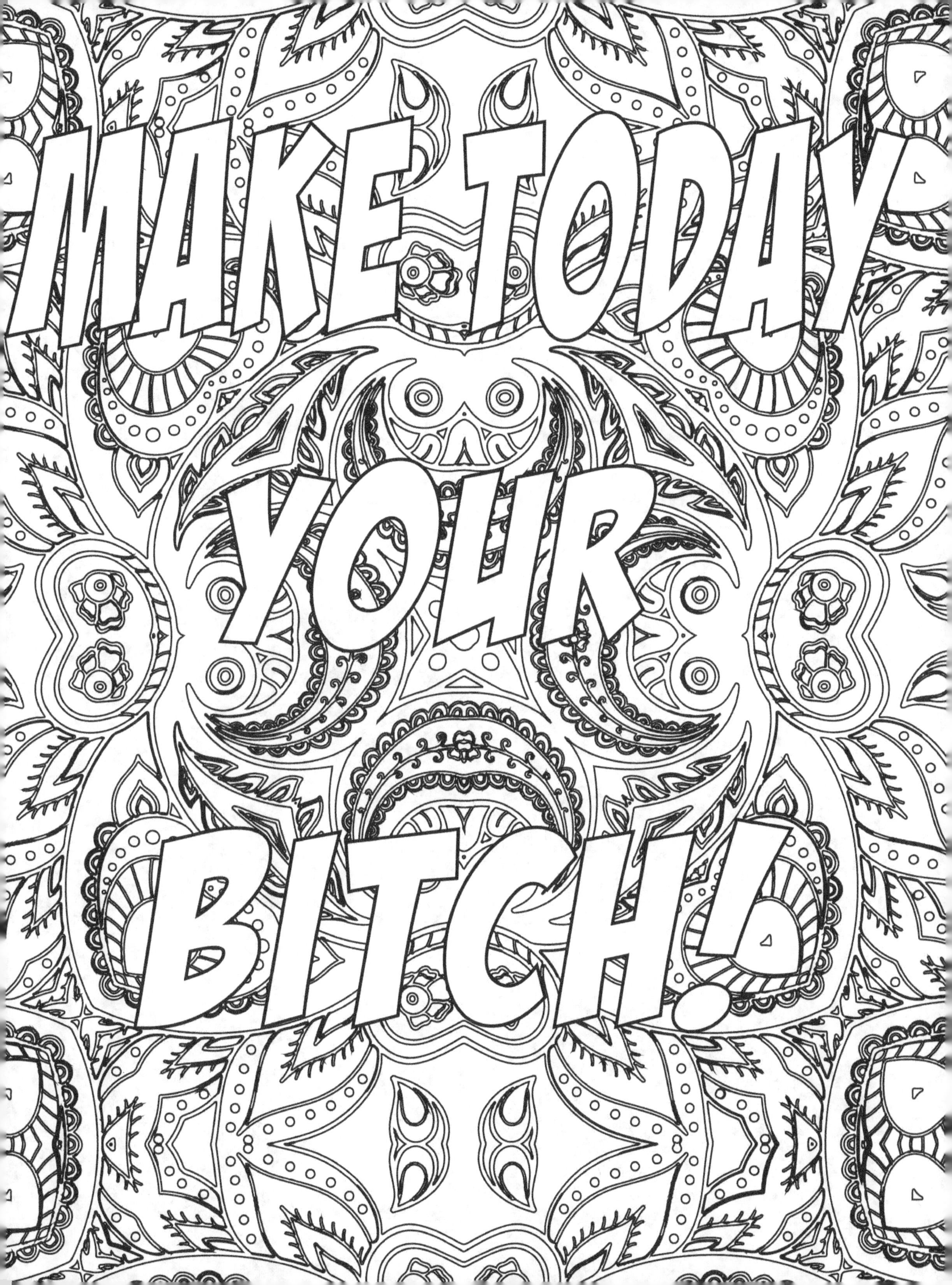
MAKE TODAY
YOUR
BITCH!

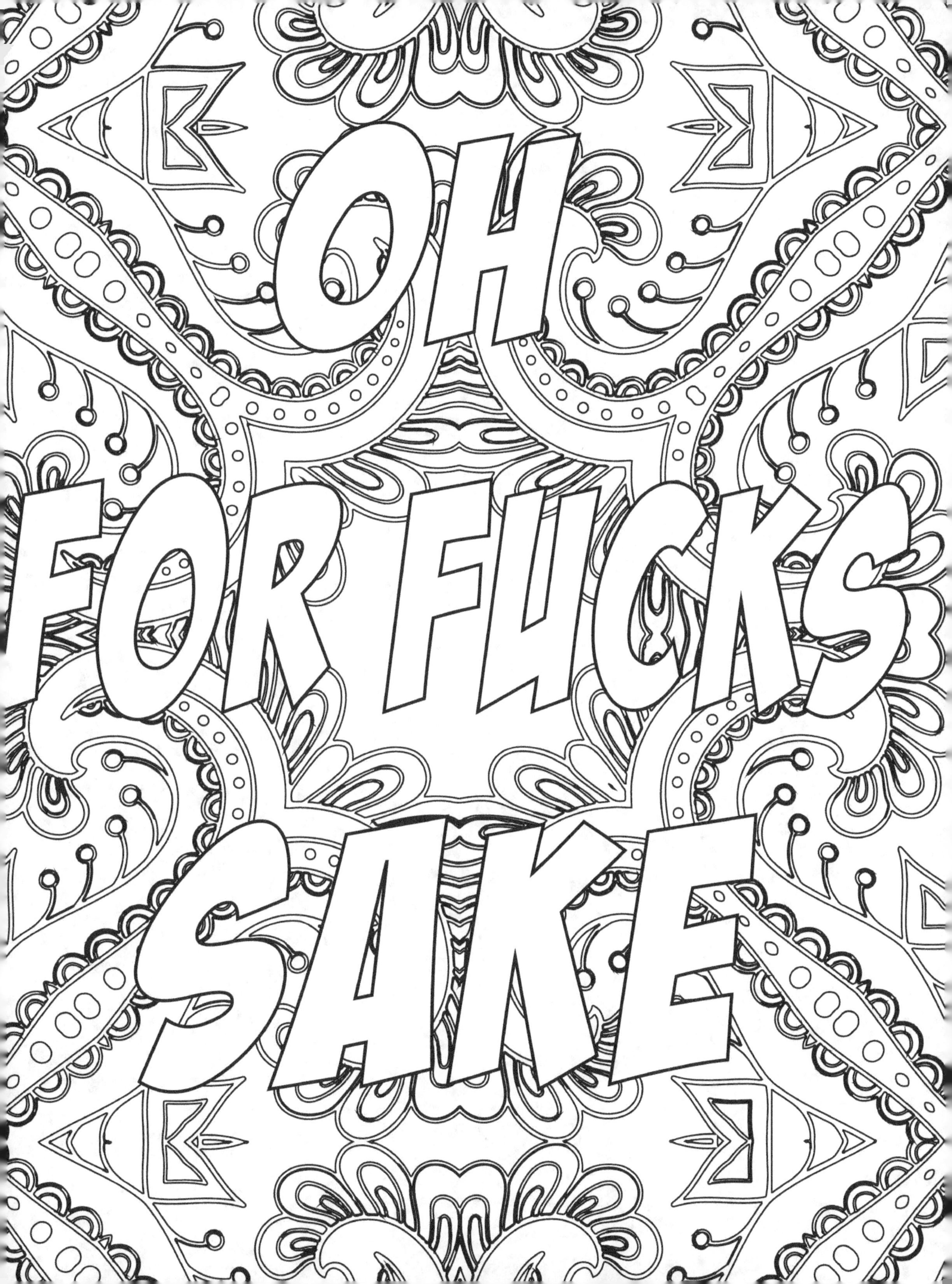
OH
FOR FUCKS
SAKE

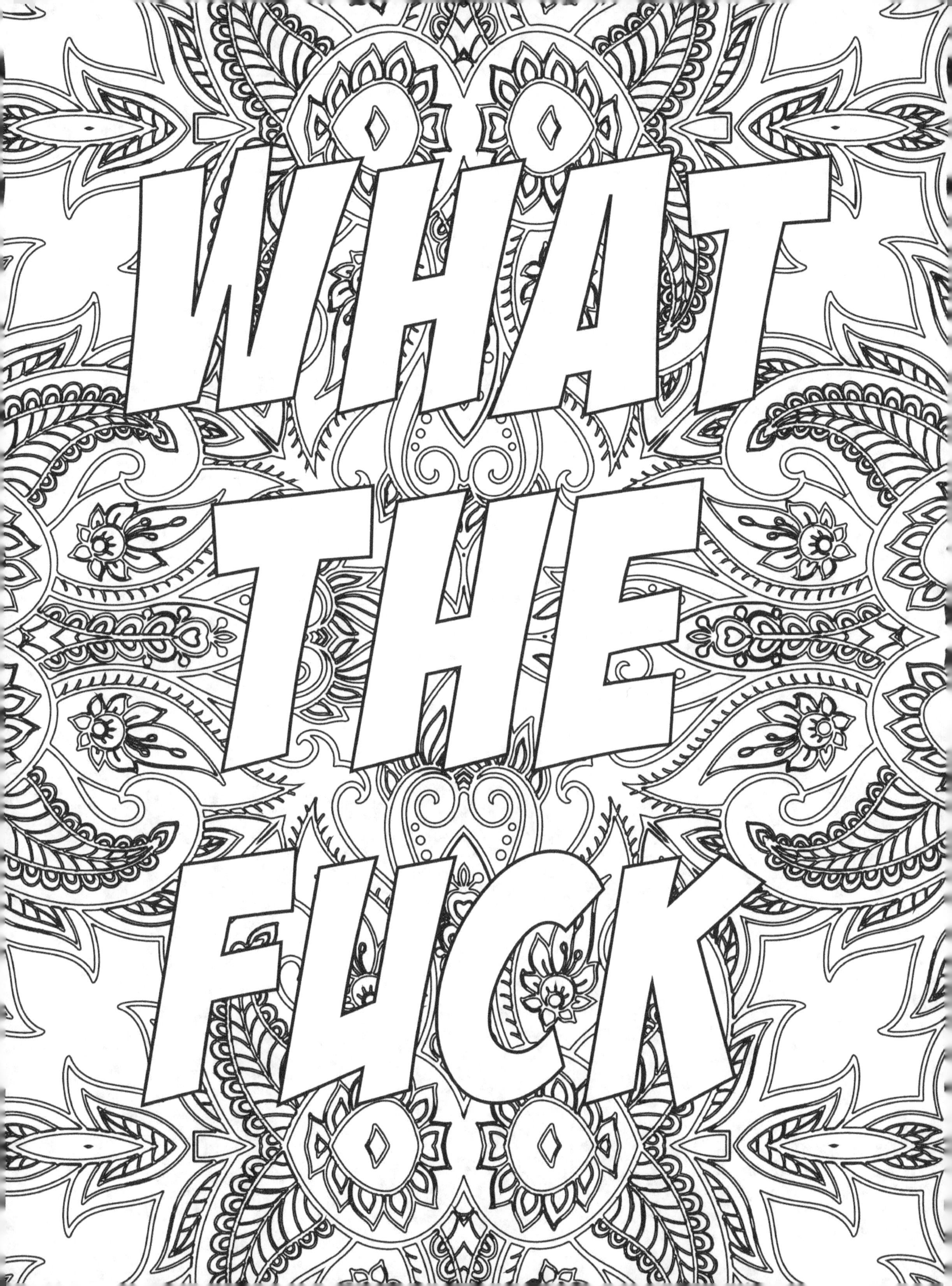
WHAT
THE
FUCK

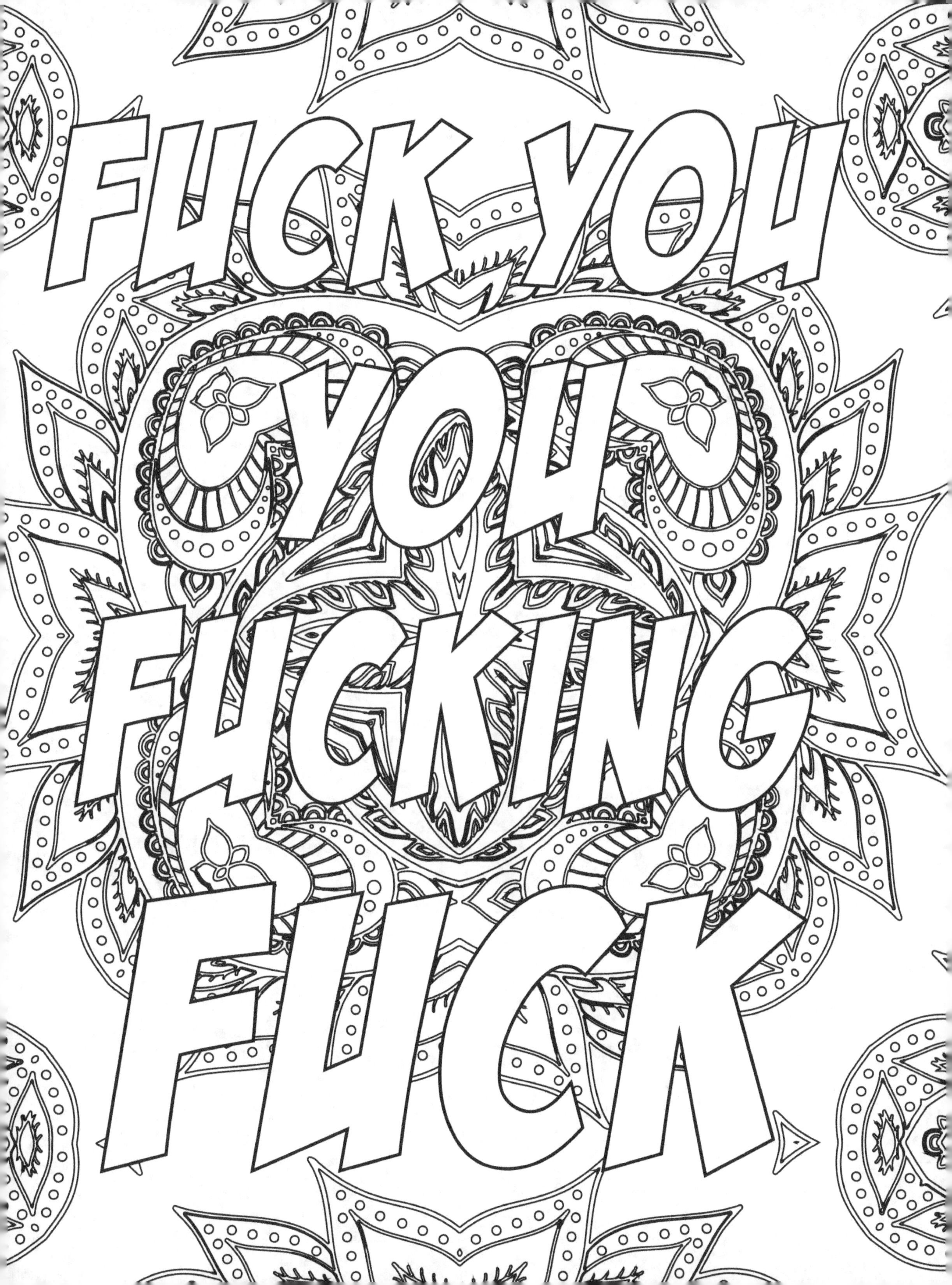
FUCK YOU
YOU
FUCKING
FUCK

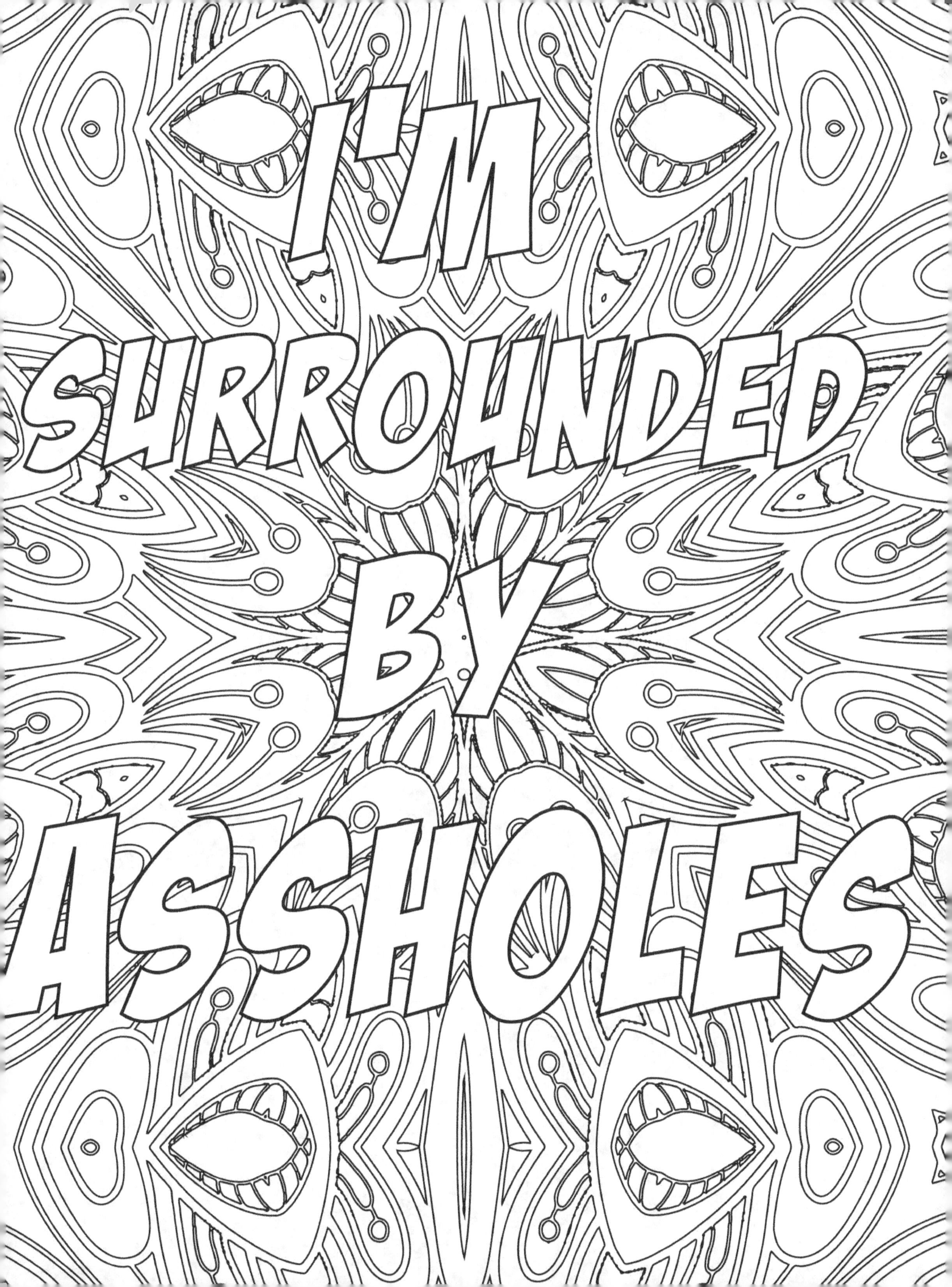
I'M
SURROUNDED
BY
ASSHOLES

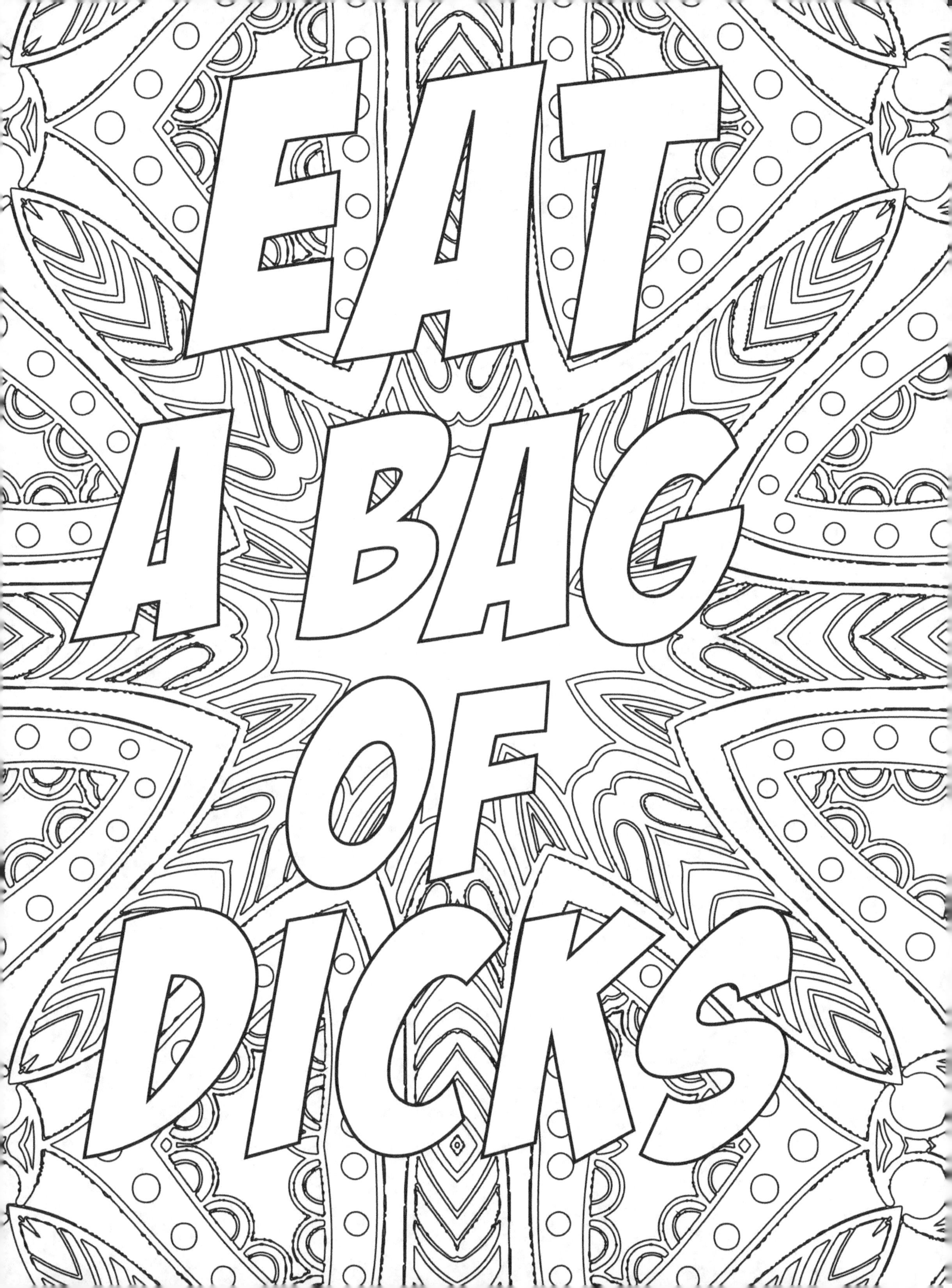
EAT
A BAG
OF
DICKS

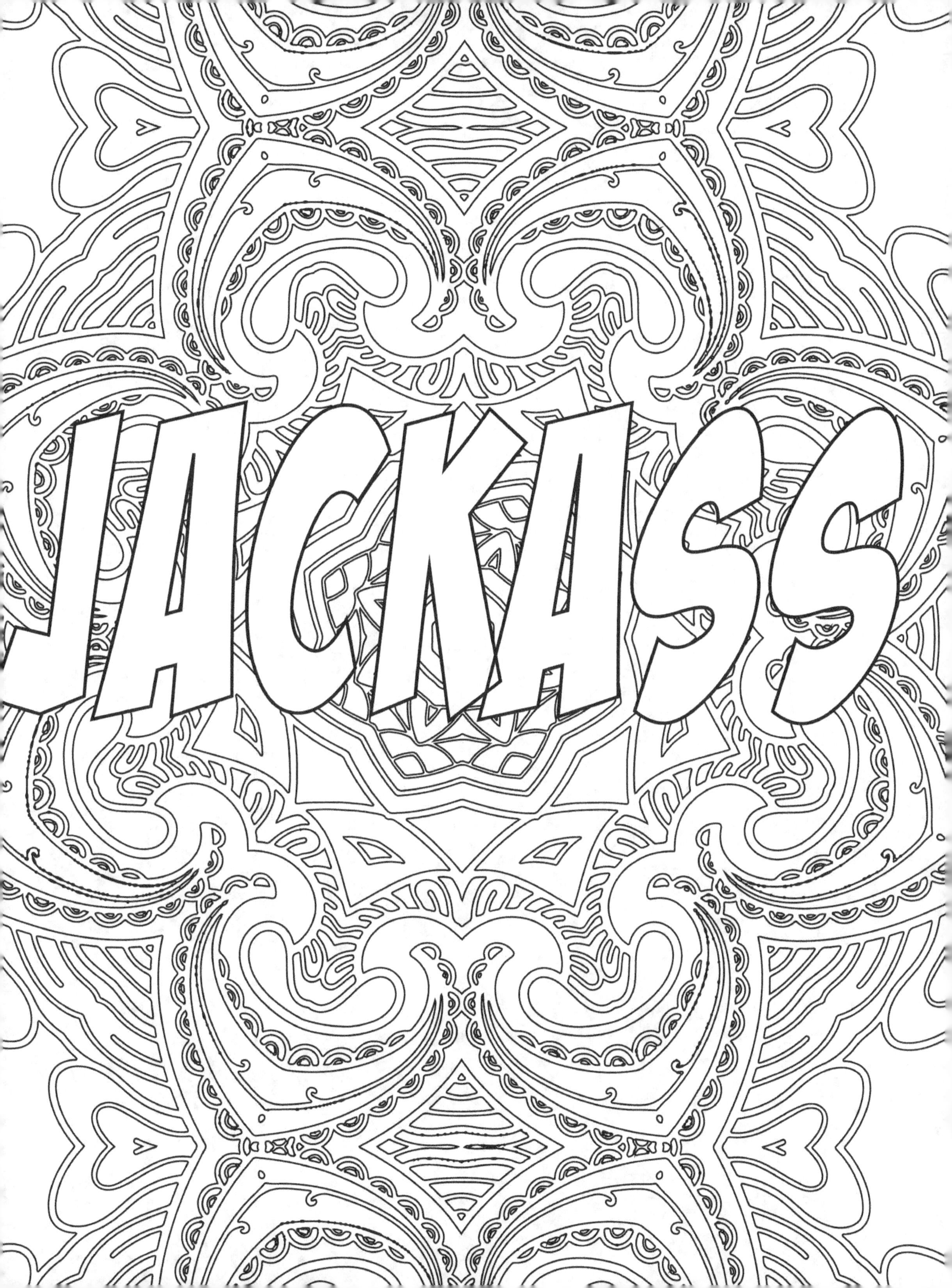
JACKASS

FUCK
YOUR BAD
VIBES

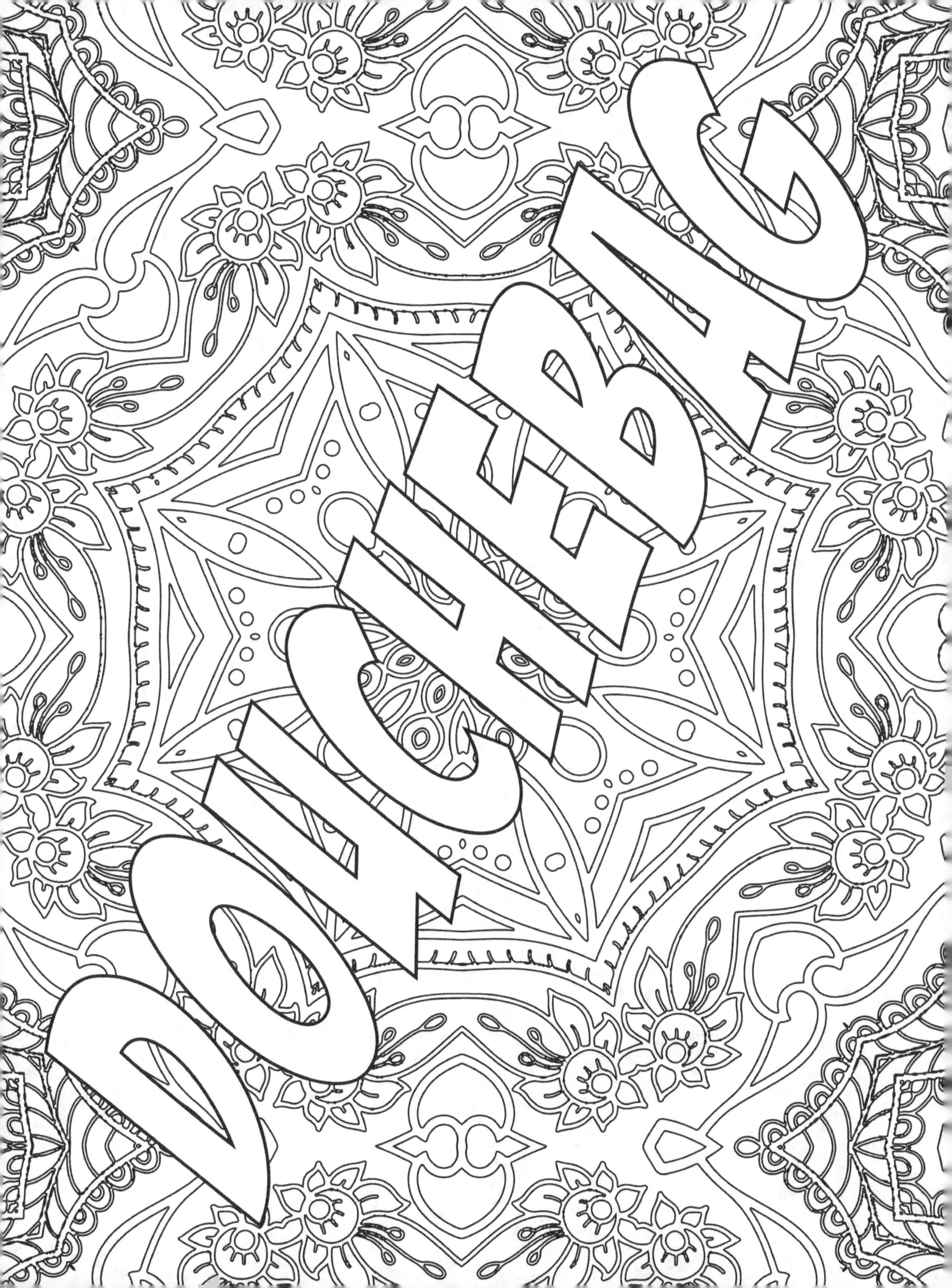
DOUCHEBAG

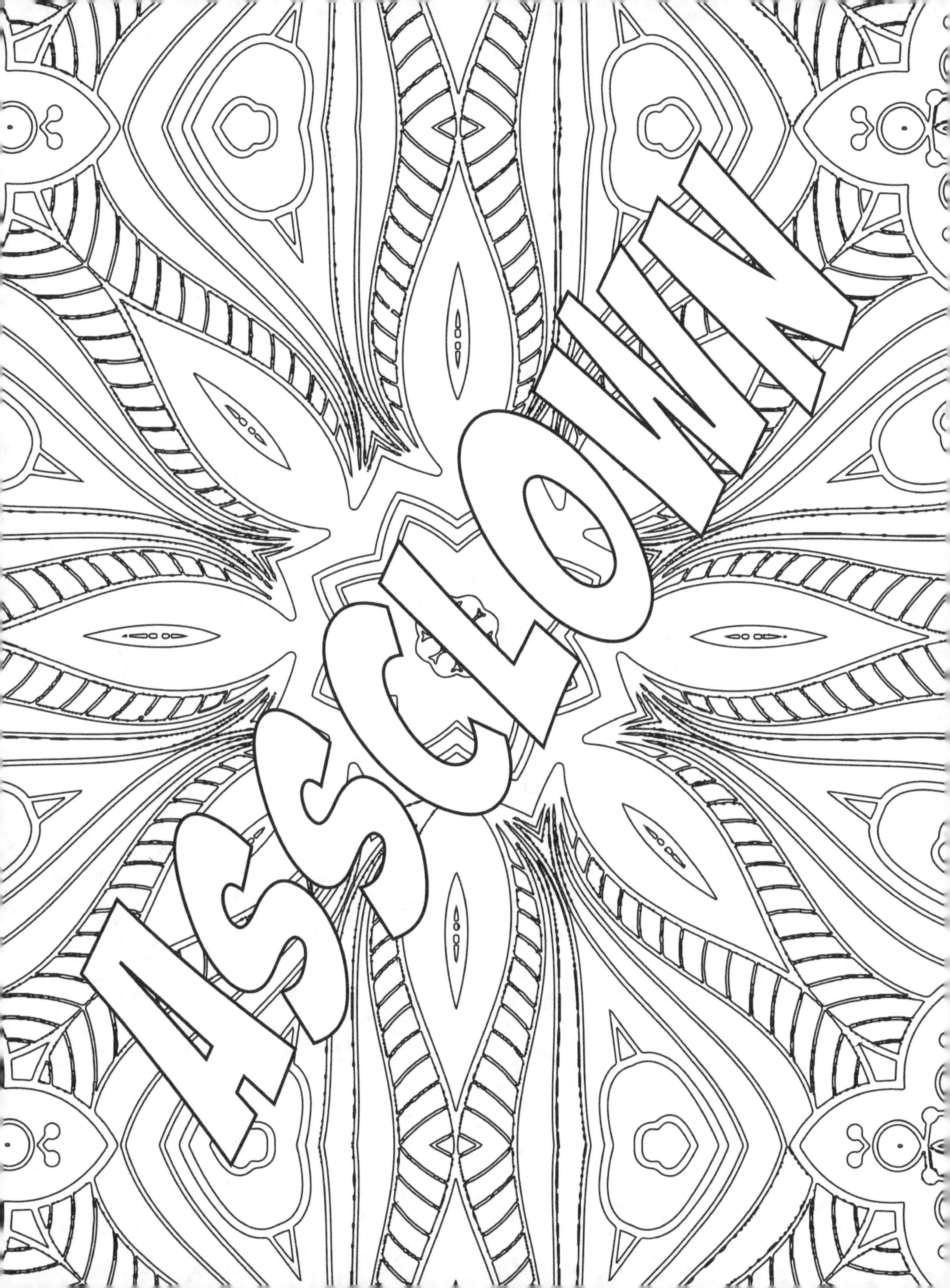
ASSCLOWN

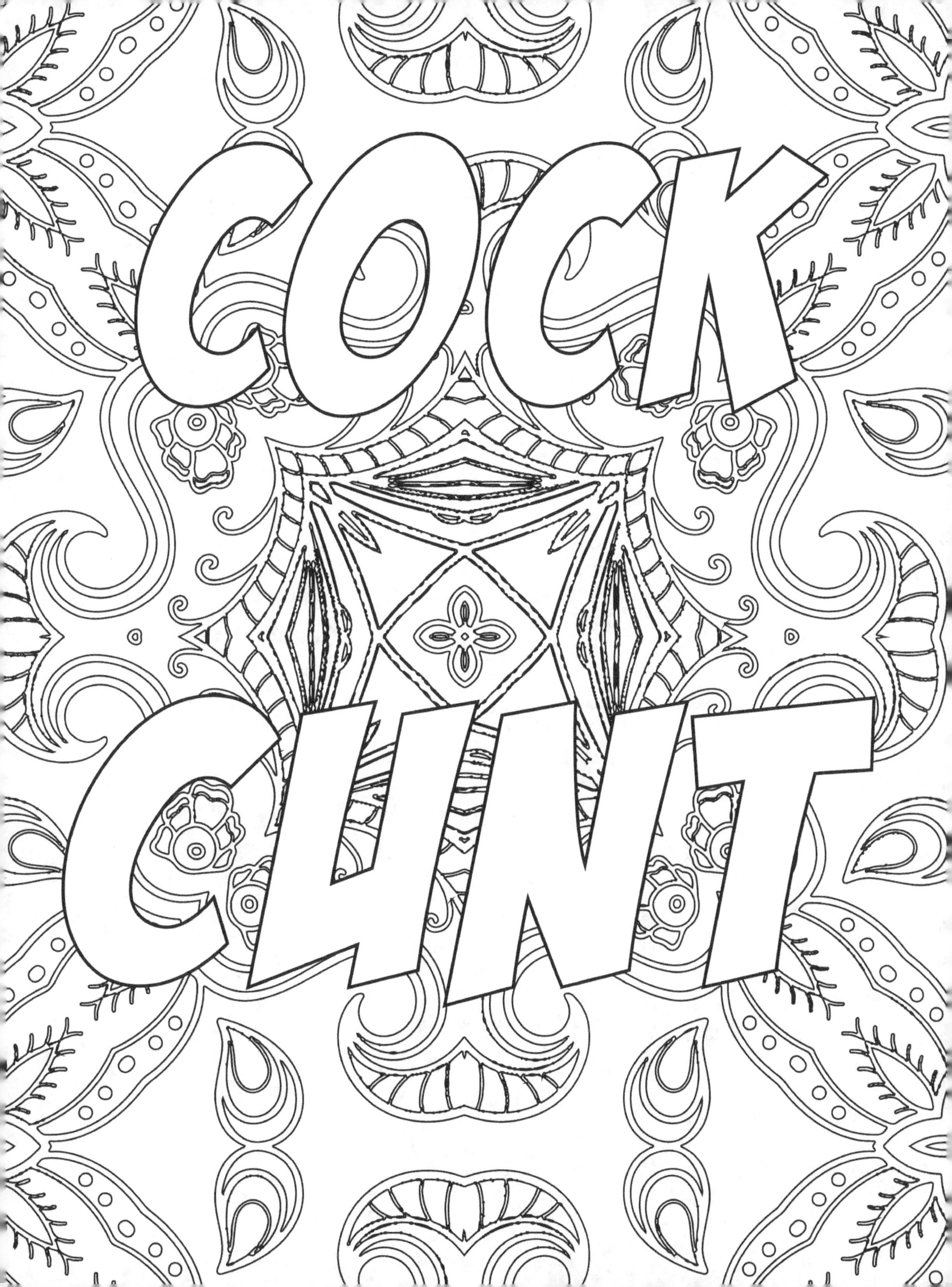
COCK
CUNT

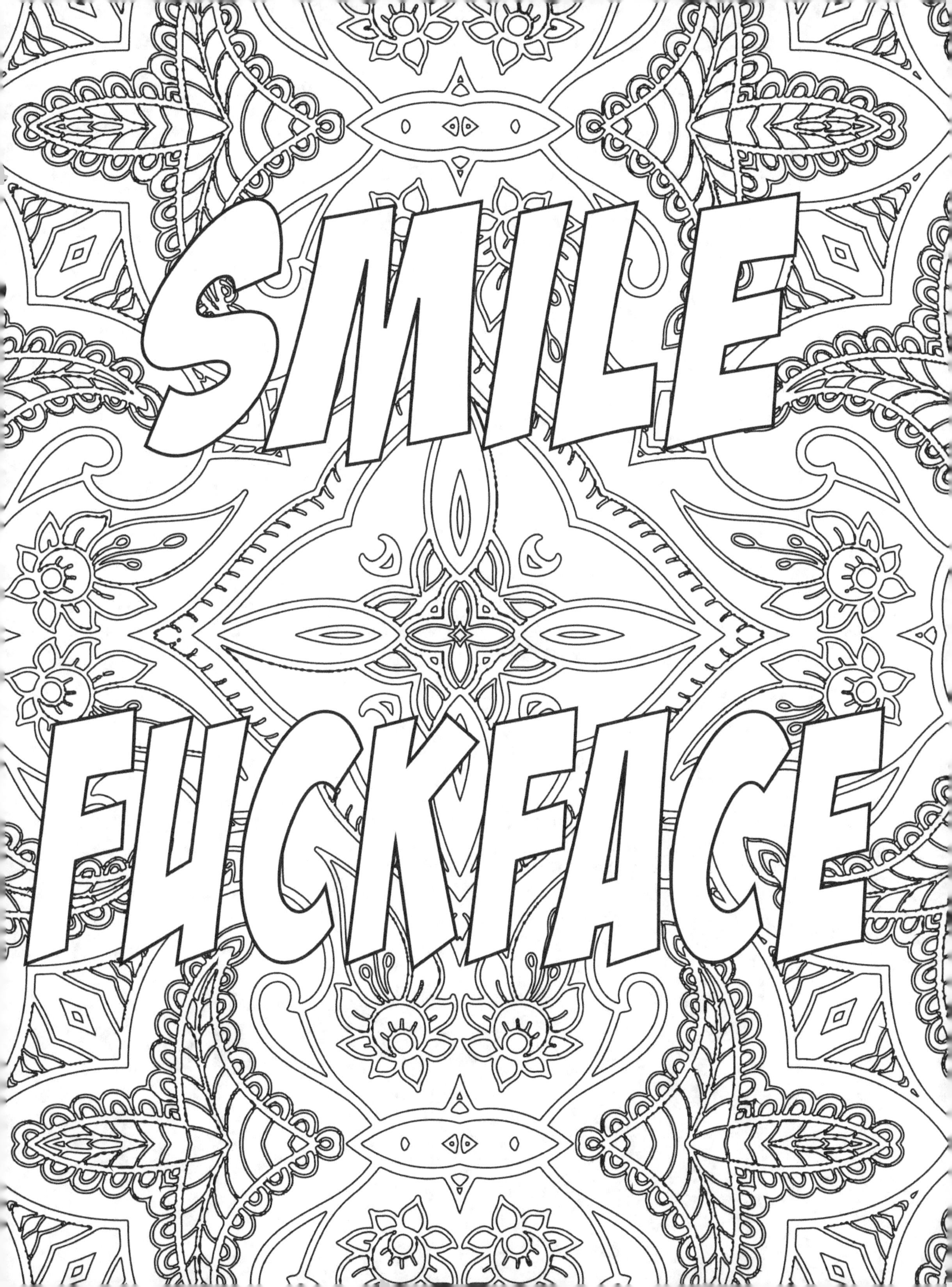
SMILE
FUCKFACE

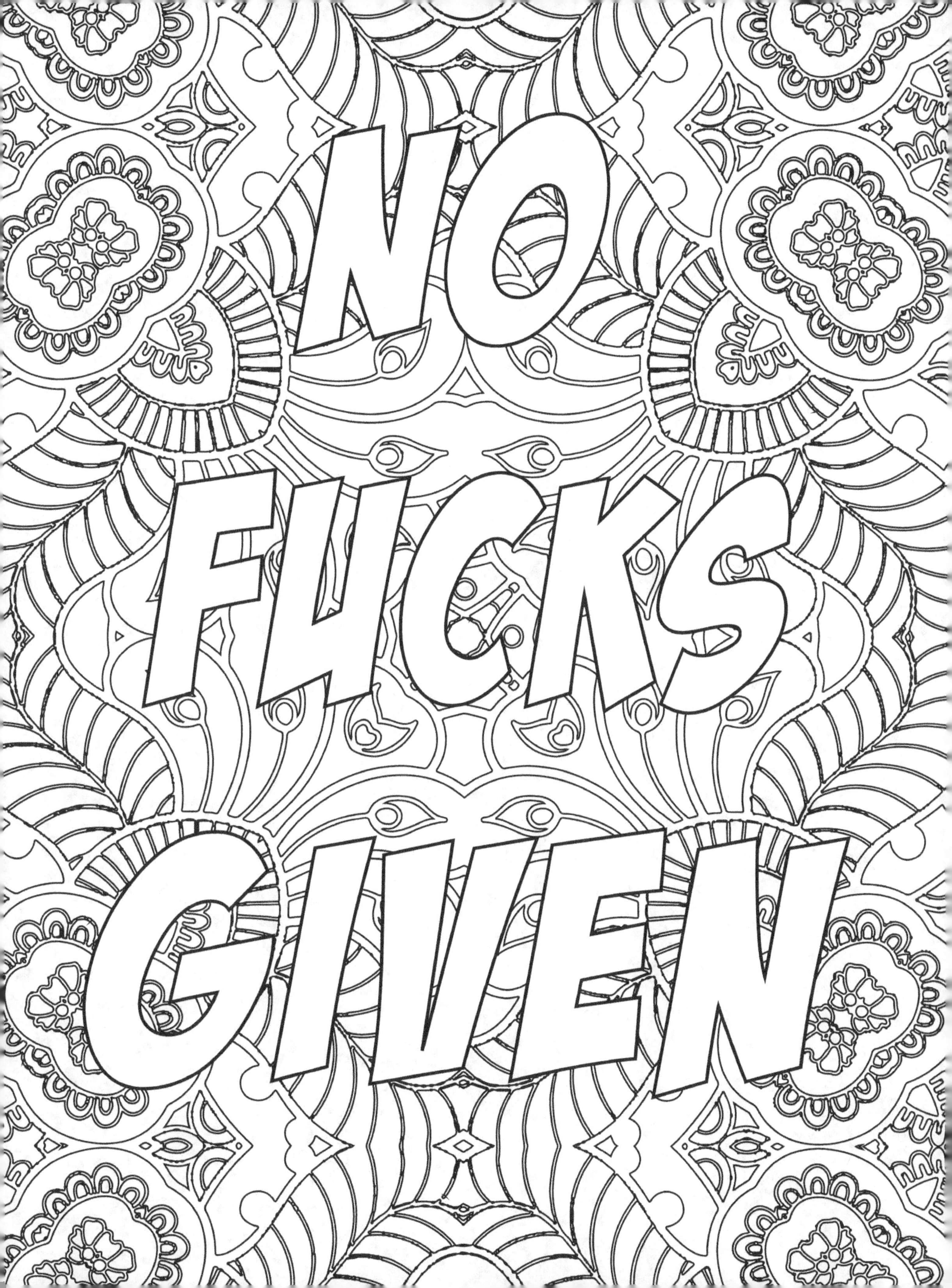
NO
FUCKS
GIVEN

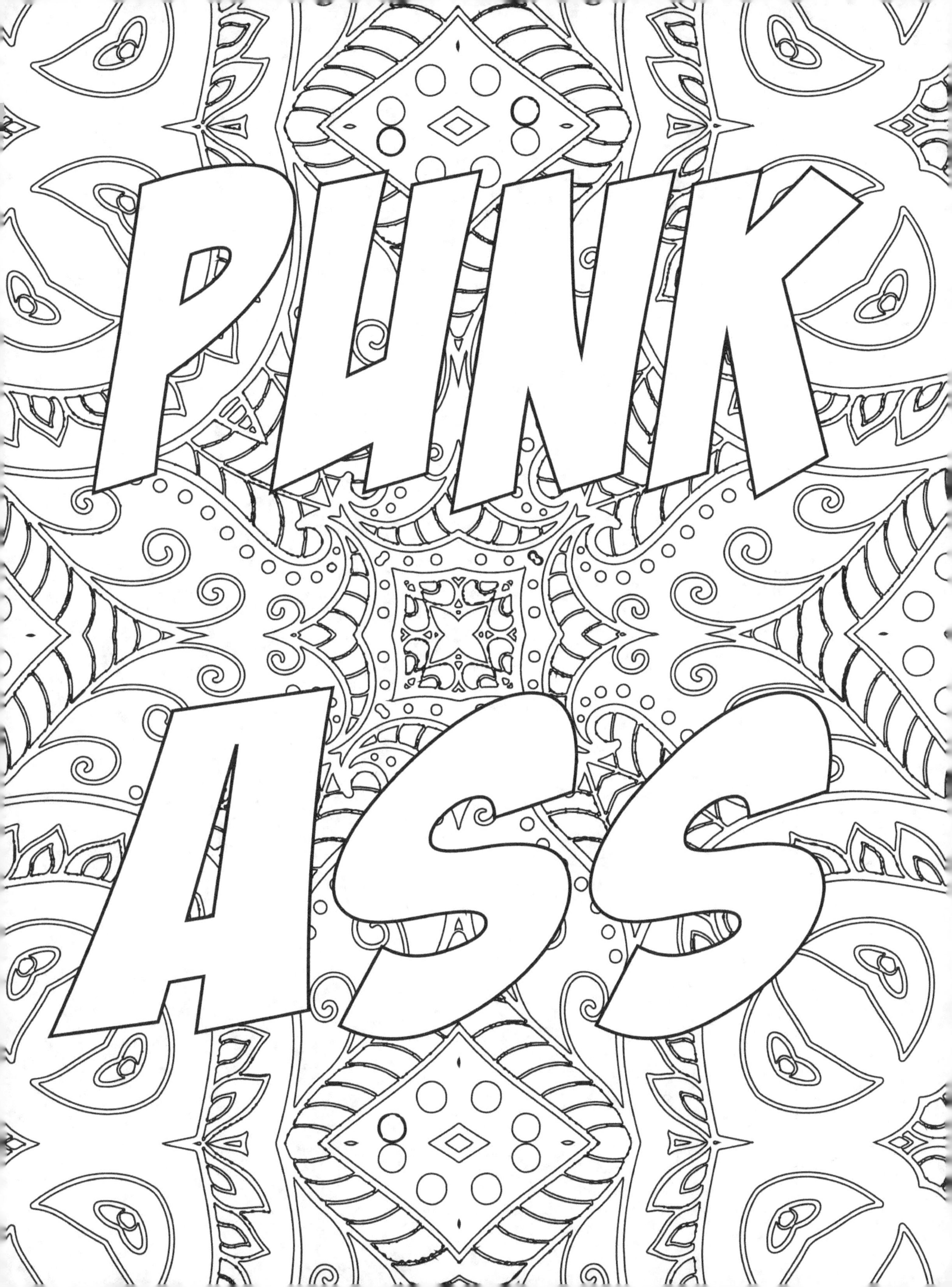
PUNK
ASS

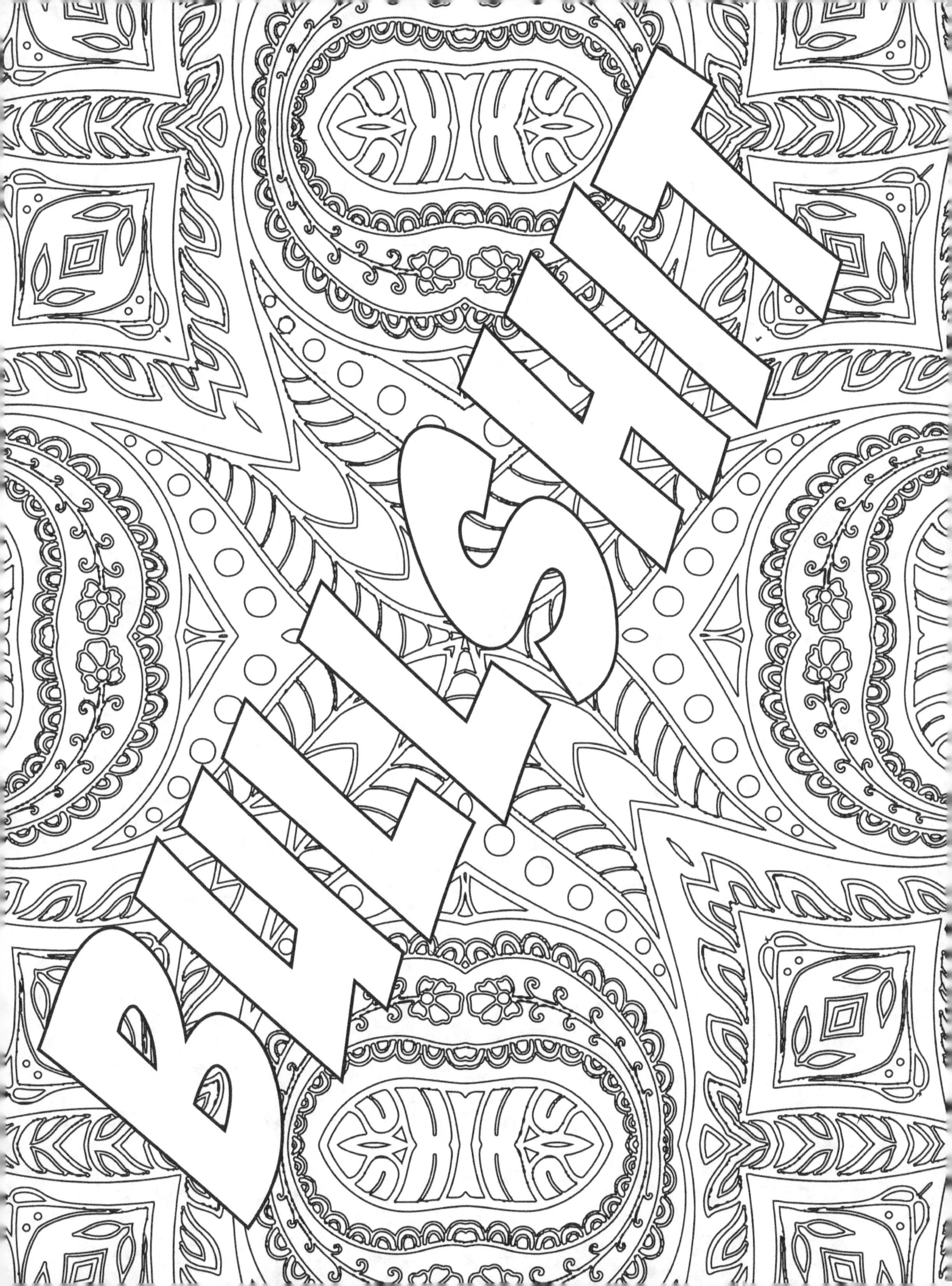
BULLSHIT

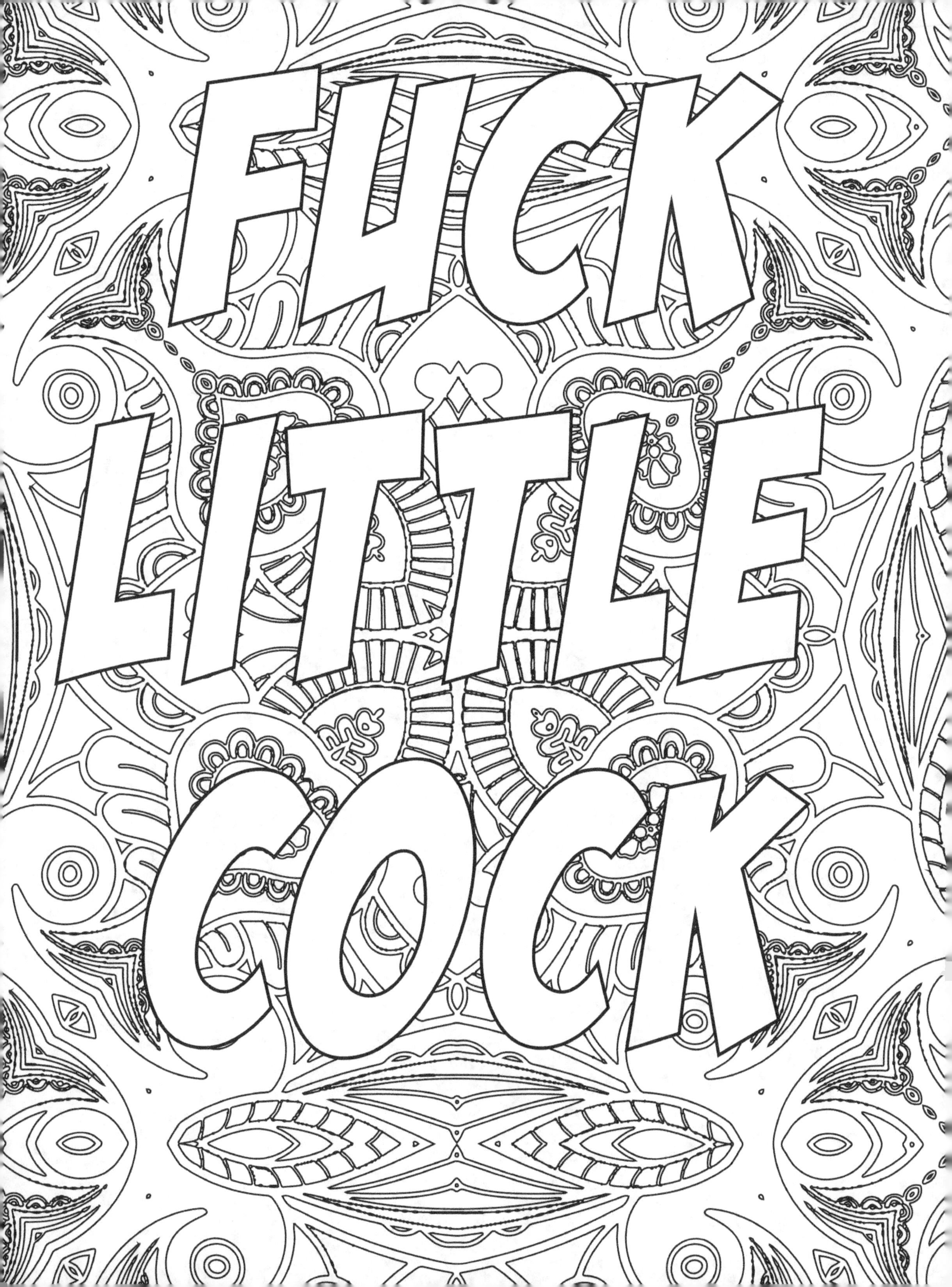
FUCK
LITTLE
COCK

www.ingramcontent.com/pod-product-compliance
Lightning Source LLC
Chambersburg PA
CBHW081539220526
45467CB00010B/3256